When the Water Came:
Evacuees of Hurricane Katrina

Interview-poems by Cynthia Hogue
Photographs by Rebecca Ross

When the Water Came: Evacuees of Hurricane Katrina
The Engaged Writers Series
University of New Orleans Publishing
Managing Editor, Bill Lavender

http://unopress.uno.edu

ISBN: 978-1-60801-012-7
Price: $24.95
Library of Congress Control Number: 2009940209

Printed in China.

To Jim, Deborah, Mimi, Victoria,
Lawanda and Sean, Catherine, Ardie,
Richard, Emily, Kid Merv, Sally, Freddie,
and all the many that
Hurricane Katrina launched
into a changed future

When the Water Came:
Evacuees of Hurricane Katrina

Table of Contents

8   James Davidson

18   Deborah Green

26   Miriam Youngerman Miller

36   Victoria Green

44   Lawanda and Sean Scott (Their Anniversary, Their Story)

53   Catherine Loomis

66   Ardiss "Ardie" Cooper (Direct Hit at Diamondhead, Mississippi)

74   Richard Lyons

80   Emily Dygert

90   Kid Merv, Some Jazz

98   Sally Cole

108   Freddie Munn, Jr.

116   List of Plates

125   Acknowledgments and Notes

When the Water Came:
Evacuees of Hurricane Katrina

James Davidson
(artist)

1

Months before Katrina, I started having dreams
of being in flood water over and over.
They were not bad dreams, not scary,
but in each dream I was chest deep
in water making my way to an exit
or an entrance to higher ground.
A lot of people were helping
each other get together
up to higher ground so
there was no fear.
Then I'd wake up.
Our dreams are so peculiar.
        You're in a strange place
                and wonder why you're there,
but you go along with it.
I had that dream many times.
Started in May and went on until
early August and then it stopped.
I guess if I didn't get the message
by then I wasn't going to.
It never dawned on me
my dreams were telling me
something. I've thought about
what if it registered, Uh-oh,
something dreadful
is going to happen, but it didn't
        so I don't know if I'd have
                done anything differently.

2

The day we evacuated,
the Sunday before Katrina,
I didn't want to leave
because every year there's a hurricane
going to come near New Orleans
and it never does.
It's hard to determine
the logic of weathermen,
to believe their predictions.
That's how they make
their money, you know, scaring us.
Saturday night the weatherman
said, It's going to be a Category 5.
        I thought, *That's* scary.
                But we'd heard it before.

In the morning Bob wakes me up,
We have to get out of here. Yeah, okay.
We've got to go. There were cops
everywhere. It was bumper to bumper.
We drove all the way to Memphis.
CNN showed all those people
trying to get up to the I-10 overpass
and I said (you don't want this on tape),
Fuck. I just don't believe it.
I'd had so many of those dreams
and then to see that water pouring
into the city and people stuck there.
It was like watching a bad sci-fi movie.
        Your mind tells you,
                This can't be real.

3

Earlier that year residents along the 17th Street Canal
had water welling up in their back yards.
They called the Levee Board, City Hall,
the Corps. Nobody cared.
Someone told them, A water main broke.
What it was
            was the dirt levees
                    were crumbling.
New Orleans sits on a big sponge.
This disaster took 300 years to make.
We couldn't go back before October.
There was no power, no gas.
Our neighborhood looked okay—
Bywater is two or three feet higher
            than the Ninth Ward and that
                  made all the difference,
two or three feet—
but there were troops everywhere.
They'd wave to us with their guns.
It was all quite friendly
and creepy. We were anxious
to get back for our cats
            which we'd left with
                  food and water enough
for a week. They were mighty skinny.
We will never know
how those cats survived.
The city is like a war zone.
Dark everywhere at night.
Whole neighborhoods *gone*.
            I saw a special on "Sixty Minutes"
                about the old New Orleans,
but it was the myth:
how it was one big party, musicians
on every street corner, booze
all the time. I was so angry
because that city never existed.
That isn't the city we lost.

Deborah Green
(Winn-Dixie employee: meat department, retired)

1

I listened to the wind all night. 5 a.m.
my mother hollers, Y'all better move your cars
'cause the water is coming up and up.
People were floating their mattresses
to the Dome with their little bitty children.
You better feed them children
before you leave, I called.
I'm gonna make y'all sandwiches.
     And I did that.
          Must have been an angel
             speaking through me.

That was the last meal
them children had for 3 or 4 days.
Something just told me,
I can't go to the Dome. *Uh*-uh.
One of my friends worked for Charity
Hospital, and she was sent
with a boat there to get the sick.
The man steering *made* her
     get out at the Dome.
          That was very . . .
            People was so *dirty*.

Girl, I ain't never thought
you were at that *Dome*, I said.
Oh, people got cold-hearted
being there without food or water.
My friend said, Debby, I looked at the things
going on there—people urinating everywhere,
the old dying, *children* getting raped—
and prayed to the good Lord,
    whatever you want me
        to do, I'll do it. *Please*
          get me out of this.

She was on dialysis so she wasn't
urinating. That held her calm.
Afterwards, the police chief who cried
to the press claimed he'd lied about it all.
Those stories are the *Lord's* truth.
At night it was pitch dark and *hot*.
Tuesday my brother walked through dirty water
all the way uptown from downtown
        to check on us. He had a long stick
           and a rag tied round his head.
                He looked like *Joseph*.
We said, Look at *Joseph*. That water stayed
a *long* time. The last time I heard
the Mayor talk on the television,
he was cussing and crying at the *same* time:
We need *help* here!
My girlfriend who lived in the Lower
9th Ward drowned. That water came up
so *fast*. Didn't give people a *chance*.
      The ones that made it
           was on the Lord's grace.
                I seen angels so I know.

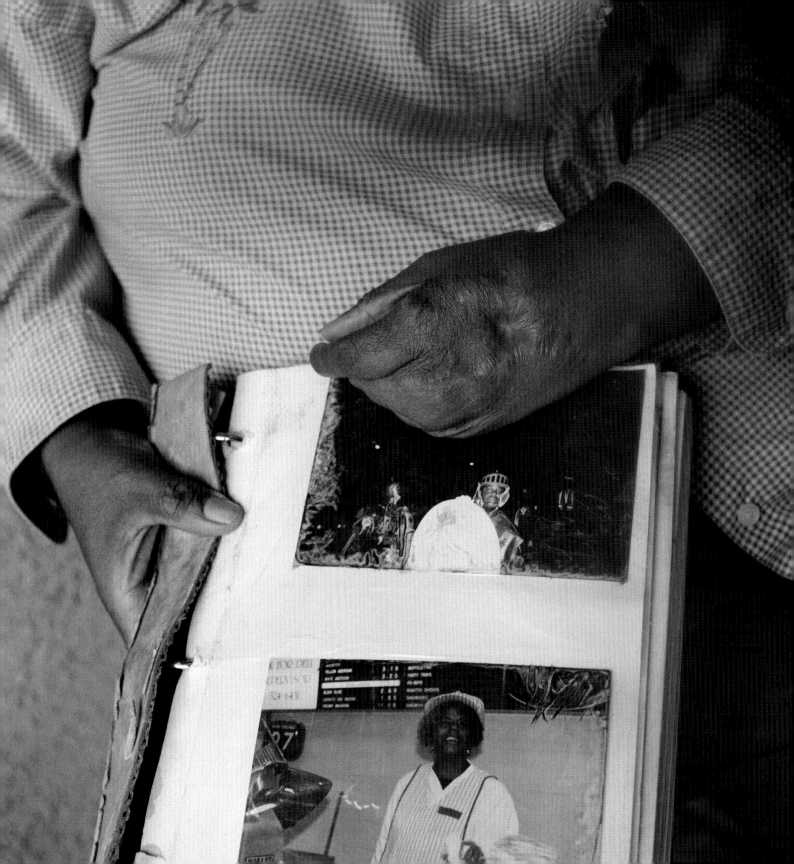

2

I dated a rich man after my divorce
from Clarence's father. Here I am.
Oooh, I was looking hot. One night
I couldn't sleep in his bed, I don't know why,
so I slept downstairs on the sofa.
When I woke in the morning—
you know how you can feel someone
in the room looking at you—
he was in the recliner with tears
        pouring down his cheeks. Baby,
            what's wrong, I asked.
                "By 8 a.m. you'll be dead."
Now what you talking about?
I did not move when I saw two guns
in his pockets, a .357 and a .22.
He took the .357 and fired.
I put up my hands to cover my face.
Oh, I cried. The bullet went through my hand,
my mouth, and the back of my head.
I tried to run but he'd locked the door,
so I sank to the floor and curled up.
        He said, You still alive?
            and shot me again
               but the .357 (brand new)
jammed so he shot me twice
with the .22 before it jammed too.
Then he hit my head with a brick
but my thick hair protected me.
When the police came—
I do not remember this—
I looked up, *Why, you come with angels.*
They fastened round me looking grim,
but when I left ICU two weeks later
        those angels was dancing
            up and down just like this
               with their wings spread.

3

By Sunday my mom said, C'mon.
I'm putting a sign outside the window
to come get me. They airlifted us
one by one from the balcony.
I was so scared when I had to crawl
out of the harness into the helicopter,
but the man said, *Just look at me*.
And it was all right. At the airport,
I went to Emergency with my bad heart.
I told my mamma, Y'all wait for me
right here, but my people was told
I had left, so they took the next plane out.
When I came back from the doctor
my *family* was gone. I shouted,
            Why did y'all tell my people I left?
                    Y'all shouldn't *do* things like that.
                            Now I lost my *family*.
I boarded the plane by myself—
didn't even know it was going
to Phoenix, Arizona—and guess who
I found? Clarence! Look at my *baby*!
I screamed. It was 4 a.m.
My son had not slept
because he thought I was dead.
He has a nervous thing
but he's coming along. My uncle
died last June. Never was sick
a day in his life, but he had a stroke
and didn't know it. People dying
from Katrina. I heard of a young woman
who killed herself and her children.
            She was depressed. *Yeah*.
                    So there is still a lot
                        going on. *Mmm-mmm*.

Miriam Youngerman Miller
(professor emerita)

1

The story that hasn't been told
is the destruction
      of the middle class
            of New Orleans.
All you heard was *poor black people*
and Barbara Bush saying
      they're better off because
          they didn't have anything
anyway. So who cares?
That made me think,
      The apple falleth
          not far from the tree,
and we can see what
Mrs. Bush has raised and
      we can see where
          they got it from.
The middle class, the middle class
residential neighborhoods all over the city—
      Lakeview, Mid-City, Gentilly,
          Tremé, New Orleans East—
were completely destroyed because of
the insurance situation. The cap on flood
      was $250,000 and prices had gone
          well beyond that.

McMansions were built
and people financed them to the hilt
       and homeowners' insurance declared
            that all the damage was flood
and refused to pay out.
People who paid through the nose
       were left with way high
            mortgages far beyond
their insurance sums
and so they're ruined.

We moved to Vista Park in Gentilly in 1990.
There were 400 households of every sort of person—
       white, black, creoles of color,
            Southwest Asians, East Asians,
Hispanics, many university people.
We lived right next to
       the London Avenue Canal
           where the floodwall breached.
One fellow had a three-foot alligator in
his swimming pool. That's how
       destroyed the area was.
           I saw the picture of this poor,
misbegotten alligator that got lost
being dragged out and relocated to a more
       salubrious place for alligators.
           This story has not been told.

2

Many of us in New Orleans
had flood insurance, but thought coverage
            came only from the government
                        which capped what
we could insure our structures for.
I did not know and few of us knew
            that some companies underwrote
                        excess coverage. I paid
flood insurance with my mortgage in escrow.
I never saw the paperwork annually.
            I thought my agent was
                        raising my limit with inflation
because I told him to
but he didn't do diddly.
            I was covered for one third
                        of the actual value of my home.
Homeowners insurance refused to pay
anything for the contents.
            They said it was all flood damage
                        which they don't cover.
The water came after the wind.
It was hard to tell
            unambiguously what was wind
                        and what was water damage.
I had plenty of insurance but
like everyone else I
            didn't get anything
                        to speak of.

I did receive $4,000 for
"alternative living expenses."
        You can get this sum for
                a mandatory evacuation.
We had that, but my company,
the evil Travelers, said, No,
        you left because of
                a non-covered peril, a flood.
I said, No no no no no no.
There was no flood.
        There was a hurricane in the Gulf
                and the flood did not occur
until after the hurricane passed.
Therefore you are on the hook
        for my alternative living
                expenses. Please remit.
I evacuated to Baton Rouge,
and knew my house was ruined
        because I saw it on CNN under water.
                They showed that shot again and again.
The tanks from the Shell station
on the corner spread their iridescence
        through that filthy water everywhere
                and I knew it was all over.

3

I didn't get back until Mardi Gras.
It took awhile to screw up my courage.
          Edward and his wife came with me
               to see what was what.
There was no salvage, so I thought,
just take a look. It was all gone—
          yearbooks, diplomas, family pictures,
               medieval manuscript pages, medieval coins
I collected of each of the medieval King Edwards
for my son, my mother's mid-century modern,
          which is now getting collectible—
               everything. Everything.
The only thing I got back:
I hid my jewel box so well during the 1995 flood
          I never found it again.
               I called the Jewish Federation
to gut the house, and I said,
I'm an old lady, will you help me?
          And they said, Yes,
               but they cleared the house out,
said someone else would gut it.
Operation Noah called me to arrange to gut
          the house. Then they asked, Are you born again?
               And I said, Is this the Jewish Federation?
I thought I was dealing with the Jewish Federation.
No, they were Southern Baptists! I said,
          I am not baptized.
               I am not saved.
But they told me they would still gut my house,
so I said, Fine, whatever.
          Thank you. Those Southern Baptists
               walk the walk, I will say that.
They found my jewel box and did not steal it.
So now I have my diamond again.

Mardi Gras was really quite nice.
Edward and his wife got into the spirit
            quickly. They dressed as
fucking ninja, that was their costume.
Elaine went to an adult toy store
            to make nunchucks out of
                        two dildos and nipple clamps.
They had their little black outfits on,
and Elaine took a video of herself
            nunchucking
                  at Mardi Gras.
When I turned up Charlotte Drive to go home,
you know, a last time, I passed my next door neighbor,
            the one closer to Fillmore than I.
                        There was a big sign in front—
"This house sheltered a family for forty years"—
and when I saw it I cried.

Victoria Green
(mother of four)

1

We always talked of The Big One,
but I had not heard of Katrina.
Hurricanes come and go.
My friend phoned, They're telling people
to leave, but not to go to Mississippi.
Storm's going to hit there.
Take a plane or train or bus
and go west go west.
      You got somebody's kids?
          Don't try to take them home.
             Bring them with you and get out.
Honest to God, I did not have $1
in my pocket or any plan.
I did not have a car (I don't even drive).
I had my elderly mother,
my 4 kids, youngest was 8 months
and I had 2 diapers for her,
my husband home from jail
on some minor charge which by
      a miracle he got out of two days
          early because of an error or
             something, my deaf uncle
Little Mervin who lived near us,
and his son who had a wife and 3 children,
and a baby my cousin was watching—
we called her Baby X because
my cousin didn't even know
her last name—and one car
wasn't going to do it for all of us.
My uncle said, "I can't go to Texas
      with $5!" None of us had any money,
          so we all went to sleep Saturday
            without deciding what to do.

I woke at 4 a.m. My antennae
were up. Something touched my lids.
Mamma? I called. My mother
slept lightly because your subconscious mind
knows something's going on.
Mamma, I said, we gotta go.
People ask, *Why didn't you leave before?*
They don't understand New Orleans'
        anatomy. New Orleans period.
              This was our *home*. We *always*
                  stay. That's what we do.

At 5 a.m. my uncle Big Mervin
who lived over by the Esplanade Ridge
called to say they'd come pick us up.
We talked of meeting by where I was raised
in the 1400 block of N. Robertson
down the street from Circle Food in the 7th Ward,
but if we would have went there
we'd be in the water. We took 3 days'
clothes. My mother said, Get your babies'
        child's records and your records
              because if the water comes, um . . .
                if the water comes, um . . .

I'm sorry, I don't talk about this . . .

2

I got to be honest.
I've been through hell and back
in my life, completely, totally.
I was kidnapped when I was 3.
I lost a brother and dozens and dozens
of friends to all kinds of murder.
I was a witness in a murder trial,
and a female shot and killed
my boyfriend two years back.
        I've been jail bait,
              a teenage bride,
                        a teenage mother.
I've come through a million things,
but this particular day was
The Twilight Zone.
When we woke up, something in the air
wasn't right. Something else
was going to happen.
First reports were that the Industrial Canal
broke—one big blow for my uncle—
who lost everything. Later, later,
        the mayor say, um, they had to
              blow up the bridge. People say
                    that didn't happen, but I heard it

with my own ears. We the people
of New Orleans knew they done it
before and they do it again.
Whatever. They're *crazy*.
Next day, Lake Pontchartrain broke.
Every one of us was screaming
and hollering. If the lake was flooding
the city, we knew it'd never be the same.
These times you remember every kid
        you went to first grade with
                by *name*. You wonder where
                        everybody was, the bum
on the corner, the pickpocketers,
the little man that's always on Bourbon Street
painting the city. CNN was showing people on houses.
This was not a strange neighborhood to me.
This was *my* neighborhood.
It's where I went to school. Where
I shopped for groceries at Circle Food.
I got married at that church,
christened my children, buried my kin.
        New Orleans is the cornerstone
                for spirituality, the stomping grounds
                        for psychic ability. You don't
get on the bus and go somewhere else.
It's our culture. You'd have to be a citizen
of New Orleans to understand.
I was here a week and my mother passed.
She never had been sick.
I think any of us would trade
any charity we got to go back
to August 15, 2005 and warn all our family
that terrible storm would take everything away
        from us. But we don't
                get those chances.
                        We get what we get.

Lawanda and Sean Scott (Their Anniversary, Their Story)
(administrative assistant, fire alarm dispatcher)

1

Our anniversary was Friday. In August
we celebrate our anniversary.
We drove to Biloxi. We wasn't
paying attention to the storm.
   We wasn't paying attention.
     We went to Biloxi.
       We went on with
our lives. The casino we were at
set out in the water, and I said to Sean,
"If a storm come through,
it's going to take all of this down."
   And it sure enough did.
     The whole place swept into
       the Gulf. *On our way home*
Sean's brother called, "What you gonna do?"
"Do for what?" "A storm's coming."
And we were like . . .
But when we got home
   we went walking in the Quarter.
     We did. With another couple.
      We went on with our lives.
Saturday morning about 2 o'clock,
I woke up and saw the storm on CNN—
you know how big it was—and I said,
"Look at that! We got to go." Yeah!

In Houston, we saw CNN: "Breaking News.
Levees breaking in New Orleans."
We saw the water pouring in.
I didn't feel a thing. I was numb.
      "What are we going to do?"
          "Where are we going to go?"
We lived upstairs, so we were spared
by the water, but we were destroyed
by the looters. *They took everything.*
Everything, everything. *Every last thing*
      except, by the grace of God,
          our wedding DVD.
That was on the floor.
That was in the middle of the floor.
You know, that was our wedding.
They took the television,
      the stereo . . . they took
          the surround sound
and the microwave, and my George Foreman grill,
my son's clothes. *My daughter's jewelry.*
People was living in our house. *Mmm mm.*
While we were gone. *Mmm mm, mmm mm.*
      I said, *"Let us go then."*
          That's how we wind up *here.*

2

In New Orleans, I was fired for failure
to come back to work in the hurricane.
I had to go to court to fight it.
Didn't have no attorney.
I went based on the information
my supervisor signed documentation
that I was on vacation on this day,
          this day, this day, and this day.
                    "You had a duty to act,"
they said. "You supposed to be
on duty." So I lost that case.
When I came back out *here*,
I was terminated from my new job
for failure to report to work.
So I went back to New Orleans
and found a job but no housing.
          Too expensive. I knew
                    there was empty trailers,
but FEMA said, "We need to clean
and inspect them." New Orleans is
slow, slow, slow. *From the beginning*
my thing was, Don't go. Mmm mm.
Don't do it. I knew it wasn't time.
But hard head here, he went. [laughs]
I knew it wouldn't work out.

EMS waited 'til he drew
             on retirement, then
hired him back. Oh they knew
what they were doing.
They said, We'll hire you
back now, but at a cheaper salary.
I looked at the big picture.
I couldn't get him to see that.
"You're worth more
             than that salary.
                          You have credentials,
you have experience.
Why quit your job here,
to go back there
to make less money?
It don't add up." My thing was,
I wanted to go home.
I want to go home.

3

We went back where the levees broke at.
Heartbreaking. *Heartbreaking.*
Empty foundations. No birds, no trees.
My friend looking for his mother's house
in the 2200 block of Tennessee
found it in the 1600 block: 2216
right there in the middle of the road.
        Downtown is like Las Vegas,
            all bright lights for tourists.
Elsewhere, it's slow because of money.
Political stuff. After Katrina, the mayor
and the governor feuded because, well . . .
It was personal. It was personal.
And they were both mad at Bush. [laughs]
I think the government didn't want
to put money into the hands
        of politicians. New Orleans
            has a reputation for dirty
politicians. But people need money
to start their lives over. FEMA
did nothing for renters.
We got $2000. Period.
We've had to borrow. Now
it's a struggle. *I don't know why*
but right now home's
        not right. But I know
            to go home is right.

Catherine Loomis
(professor)

Storms follow a pattern once they start,
but Katrina moved west, not north.
Friday, I was at Sally's house watching CNN,
and we said, *That storm moved.*
On the way home, I bought all the water left
at Save-a-Center, seven gallons, and when
I saw the display of batteries at the front,
I thought, I ought to get a pack.
That small decision saved my life.
By Saturday, everyone I knew left.
I had $18, 4 cats, and 2 carriers.
Where could I go? Sunday
the sky turned an awful orange.
The whole house shook back and forth.

Monday there were 4 feet of water
along Gentilly Ridge where I lived,
which is high ground. Live Oak leaves
shredded, stuck all over like green confetti.
I swept the porch, looking for things to do.
The cats came out with me—they're all feral—
and I heard a tiny splash behind me.
Lily, short for Lilliputian,
the runt of a litter I rescued,
was gone. No sign of her.
Every day I checked to see
if she'd risen up from the water
somehow, a god-awful ritual.
I had the radio for news,

broadcast by daytime disk jockeys—
maniacal fanatics—who put anyone on air.
People stuck in attics,
people who were dying:
"I'm a diabetic with one bottle of water left.
Can anyone help me?"
This terrible information
was all we had. At first,
the water was clear. Then it turned
the tea color that swamp water gets
from tannins in bark. Raw sewage
floated up, and benzene. I did not know
about the violence with which water
moved through some neighborhoods.

I had fish in the yard.
The first living thing I saw
was a Lakeview parrot—a sign
of great good luck. Then hummingbirds,
dragonflies, a hawk blown way off track.
There was a super silence we don't have
in America—no hum of appliances,
no traffic—until the helicopters came.
I made a big *I'm all right* sign,
which I taped to my balcony
in case they were flying by, or,
someone saw me on a satellite photo.
I sat each day in Susan's white rocker
so if someone came by in a boat,

I'd make a good picture for TV.
My neighbor, Tim the Looter,
called, "I'm going out!
Need anything?" Thursday I saw
my only National Guardsmen, who said:
"They're coming for you tonight.
First they'll rape you. Then they'll
kill you. You need to come with us."
I can't get in that water.
Immune-compromised. Cancer
patient. Nope. Off they went.
Katrina arrived
      on the first anniversary
           of my second diagnosis.

I had Vicodin from the mastectomy,
which I left on the kitchen table
for looters, so they wouldn't take
anything else. One night
there was an explosion, fires
breaking out in Bywater. It looked like
all downtown was burning.
The horrible disk jockeys said,
It's Armageddon. Race war.
They made perceptions, if not
problems themselves, so much
worse. Mr. Benny, the firefighter,
and his wife Miss Suzy across the street
had a huge freezer of food,

which they had to throw away
using special firefighters' trash bags
that looked very official,
yellow with black writing.
The floodwaters were flowing.
Mr. Benny let the bags float off, and—
I know this sounds like movie timing—
just as he releases the last bag,
a helicopter drops water and MREs,
and out of nowhere comes a stream of people
for the food. A man grabs one of the trash bags
and opens it. "This ain't nothing
but meat too rotten to eat! How dare
the government do this to us!"

By Saturday, Mr. Benny and Miss Suzy
brought me shrimpers' boots. "Tomorrow,"
they said, "you follow us out."
I packed a suitcase and went to bed.
At 9:30, I heard three shots on my street.
There was a pause. Then three more,
closer, then a pause, then three more, closer.
If they found people alive,
were they killing them
with a sawed-off shotgun?
People outside of New Orleans
ask how I knew what gun was firing.
I lived in Bywater.
We heard guns all the time.

I'd write in the margin of my Riverside
Shakespeare the number of shots
and the time, and next day look in the paper.
I learned to identify different caliber weapons.
A sawed-off shotgun has a distinctive sound.
I know things I shouldn't know.
At that moment, I knew:
This is what it feels like to wait to die.
I took my flashlight, stood at a window,
and SOSed with it.
Three dots,
      three dashes,
            three dots.
To this day I can't believe
that a Coast Guard patrol saw that light
and Dave Foreman from Apex,

North Carolina in his big, goofy helmet
jumped out of a helicopter,
landed on the balcony and said:
"Everything's going to be okay now."
And then we flew through the air
like an apotheosis. "Gosh," I said,
"I'm really glad you guys still use
Morse code." This is my full
disclosure part. They don't use Morse code;
they look for blinking lights.
Having batteries for my flashlight
was the key to my rescue.
We're so lucky in this country
not to have these images in our heads:

the airport taken over by an army,
weapons everywhere. You never
want to see that in a civilian space
with which you associate happy things.
When we evacuated, we were lined up,
and they screamed, "Go! Go! Go!"
like it was a military operation.
We had to run onto the plane.
It was ATA Airlines, which the government used
to transport prisoners, so all flight attendants
were armed. I was one of 3 people
who had not been at the Superdome.
I sat beside a very chatty Uptown looter
who gave me the straight talk:

how they stole mail trucks
because they're easy to hotwire
and never stopped. How they took
truckloads to Houston and Atlanta.
All I could contribute to the conversation
was that I put Vicodin on my kitchen counter.
"Oh, baby, you so stupid!" he said.
"They're going to say, 'What's she hiding?'
and tear your place apart!"
We arrived at a Red Cross shelter
in Charlotte, and I sobbed—I had not cried—
until this woman came walking herself by
in a wheelchair, and said, "You ain't got *nothing*
to cry about!" And she was right.

I had a cot for the night, nobody around,
and I thought, Oh, thank God, it's quiet.
But I woke up thinking,
What is wrong with this picture?
Where had they put everyone,
all the sick people, the children?
I had no idea that
Charlotte's shelters were segregated!
Outside, though, there's a *stream* of people
with bags of clothes, toys,
envelopes full of money.
Everyone came to help.
That fall we had to teach classes electronically.
We're scattered everywhere, students and faculty.

Every email was heartbreak or gloom.
I'm in Memphis but my family's in Utah.
I'm taking class from a tent in the backyard.
Try to teach a play with characters lost
in a storm—*King Lear*—to hurricane evacuees.
Tell this story in blank verse sonnets or rhyme.
Like Lear, I thought to control the winds of time
by making them metric. Try teaching this play
on dial-up. Expect of your students the most.
Miss Suzy and Mr. Benny went right back.
Sally returned early, too, and cleaned
my whole apartment. Four months later,
I walked in and there's Lily sitting
on the bedroom windowsill. Lily,

who drowned. Lily
who taught herself to swim. Lily
who fed herself somehow all that time.
New Orleans asked urban planners
to look at maps and tell us where
we should and shouldn't rebuild.
"Let people live here,"
they said, and: "Don't let them
live there." If you overlay
a racial map of the city,
so many houses owned by blacks
are where no one should ever
have built neighborhoods. So now
we have exactly what we feared.

Ardiss "Ardie" Cooper (Direct Hit at Diamondhead, Mississippi)
(casino bartender)

1

This is me. This is my life.
Here is my daughter Colleen
with President Bush's Secret
Service man acting aloof.
              Here's Haley Barbour.
                        This is St. Stanislaus,
                                  pretty much leveled.
Here's my daughter's classroom in
Our Lady Academy which
they'd just built. Each year we
had to give $250 to pay for this school.
              Colleen went here from 7th
                        grade to graduation. Here
                                  it is after the hurricane.
These are all her weird friends.
They wrote plays at our house,
put them on in different classes.
Colleen and this girl combined characters—
              Alice in Wonderland, the Titanic,
                        Shakespeare and Greek myth.
                                  They were really cute.
This is graduation. The floorboards
were this far apart. We saw grass growing
underneath. Here is St. Claire's,
the school, the church, the nunnery.
              This is the Highway 90.
                        This is the beach.
                                  This is the Gulf of Mexico
backed up to Bay St. Louis
which backed up to the Jordan River.
And we flooded
right here north of the I-10.

2

Monday morning, Colleen's father
woke me about 8:30. Our backyard flooded
right up to the patio. Then the carpets started
buckling from below. I opened
the bedroom door and yelled,
         "You girls better get your
               asses up because the water is
                      coming into this house."
My daughter was in a pair of softies
and a swimsuit. Virginia had on shorts
and a T-shirt. I grabbed insurance papers,
my coin purse for tips—I was a bartender
at the casino—a little medicine,
        put them in a Mudd Bag
           I tossed in the attic.
                We had our two cats,
Virginia's cat, a Pekingese we were taking care of
for someone who'd gone to Chicago, Colleen's
goldfish that she won, which had grown
this big, and we all went to the attic and
looked down. The water rose to the top
        of the bottom window
            in the living room, my TV,
                leather sectional, double-
door refrigerator floating around so we went
downstairs and my ex broke the window
and we each crawled on the sill and jumped.
By 9:20, we're hanging on the gutters
off the roof. My ex pulls himself up,
       then Colleen, Virginia's a little
           heavy and he popped the bone
              out of his leg hauling her up.

Then he helped me—we did all this
in 5 minutes—and crawled up the peak
because the water had reached the roof.
We found a sheet of tin floating by
       that we used to keep the wind
            from blowing us off in the rain,
                and we clung close to four hours
listening to pine cones and needles
from the pine trees zing by,
watching my new Altima, my daughter's Acura,
Virginia's mother's Suburban,
and the neighbor's pickup truck playing
       bumper cars in the cove.
           Then all of a sudden the cars
              were underwater – whoosh – gone.
The girls said, We need to swim over
to a higher roof, and I said, You girls
are crazy. You see that wild boar?
A wild boar back of the house
was swimming for his life in the direction
       they wanted to go. *We're not going*
          anywhere. By 2 p.m. we sat in the
            hurricane's eye in dead calm.
My ex found a two-by-four in the water
and poked a hole in the roof,
pulled us into the attic with the animals
where we sat on the rafters until the storm
turned and pushed the water back to the Gulf.

We were across the I-10.
We weren't supposed to be hit.
On the other side of Diamondhead,
there was not one thing left—
the airport, all the people with their planes,
       their hangars,
             the yacht club—
                     everything destroyed.
My daughter's friend and his father clung to a tree.
Donnie got to the I-10 bridge,
waded to our house, and called, *Anybody there?*
Close to 6 o'clock we reached the church.
They had a grill going,
       and water, soft drinks, wine.
            A man on oxygen
                 was dying. A little girl,
I think, too. I don't know what was wrong.
The paramedics came, but no doctors.
We tried to sleep on the pews.
People coming all night,
talking and talking, no peace possible.

3

In the morning, the Baptists made breakfast.
A man who owned a bunch of McDonalds
franchises in Tuscaloosa, who didn't know
we were dirt poor, invited us to his big house,
which only lost a few trees. His hurricane
preparation was 6 bottles of water, peanut butter,
  crackers and a can of tuna.
     This man was obviously
       a big business person
but he was a mess. My daughter went
for two weeks to the land of no
electricity, no running water, no
flush toilets—Salteo, Mexico—as
president of Our Lady of the Gulf
Catholic Youth Organization with two
busloads of mostly black kids from
   St. Rose of Lima to do
     community service. A month
      after she got back, Katrina hit.
She knew just how to brush teeth
using little water, how to disinfect hands
with Listerine. She'd bought a guitar
in Mexico, which survived with our jacuzzi.
My ex had been . . . you can turn that off
and I'll tell you. Lots and lots of people
   got divorced. Lots gone crazy.
     Here is my boyfriend I met here.
      Here we are together. I wouldn't
make it without him. I should show you
a video of this guy getting deluged
and dying in his truck. My girlfriend said
she'd send me a copy but she hasn't yet.
Here is a datebook that starts the day
Katrina hit. Here is my trip across country.
  This is my story. Can you believe
     somebody has a datebook starting
      the first day of the rest of her life?

Richard Lyons
(Vietnam veteran)

1

My sister left the day before the hurricane.
Me being hardheaded . . . I didn't leave.
I went to the French Quarter with friends
for a hurricane party
and got trapped.
   Couldn't nobody get in,
      couldn't nobody get out.
At first, it was fun.
We barbecued and partied,
four blocks from the heart of the Quarter.
We didn't have no water,
no electricity. No gas, no
   nothing. The moon wasn't out.
     By 6 o'clock it was pitch dark.
Hold your hand up,
you couldn't see it.
We all ate together. We
lived together. We
found us a store. We
   broke in there, got us
     meat, charcoal. We
sat together and prayed. I was happy.
You know the 12-step program?
We say a prayer, then drink. [laughs]
It dawns on me sometimes, we
have to believe with our minds.
   Yeah, He give us strength. We
     utilize the strength real good.

Monday we heard an explosion.
It was like dynamite on the levee.
A loud explosion. Then the water came.
Anybody in their right mind left.
I'm not saying I'm not in my right mind.
       Even if I'd had a car,
            I would have stayed
anyway. Louisiana used to get a little wind
and a little rain. Why leave?
But most of the people there
didn't have cars or nothing
so they couldn't leave.
       The Governor got buses
          to transport prisoners.
How come she can't give some to the people?
It amazed me. Louisiana had no plan!
Everybody put in the Superdome,
which don't have facilities.
Why send people there? That part
     didn't make no sense.
         I got mad behind that.
I could hear the Superdome
from where I was. All kinds of people
locked in. You see that big fence
all the way around the car?
It's twenty feet high. It was like that.
     Couldn't nobody crawl up
        and get over. And somebody
have the key that opens it up
to let people out, but took off instead.
Somebody else come with bolt cutters
to open the gate. You're not going
to read that nowhere,
     'cause nobody talks
        about it. Blame the . . .
I'm going to leave it at that.

2

In July of last year my Hepatitis C
started up again. Maybe it come
from Vietnam, 'cause I was wounded
and had a blood transfusion in the army.
I don't know. One year I had a cold
and took aspirin and kept on working.
          The next thing I know,
                    I can't breathe.
I'm having a heart attack.
Doctor told me to quit smoking
but I didn't quit. He said,
*I'm going to tell you all the chemicals
in cigarettes. You embalming yourself,
'cause they use embalming fluid.*
          I've quit now. Long time ago,
                   I was on drugs. During the war.
I turned seventeen in Vietnam.
You see your brothers fall
or get blown up, you got to have
something to keep going.
We were living in the war zone.
If they keep sending guys over to Iraq
          without armor, they don't stand
                  a fighting chance. We did . . .

I think Katrina was the best thing
could've happened for us.
So many people was just hustling
in the street. That storm tried
to bring us together.
I feel sorry for the people like
       my sister who worked so hard
             to buy her house. People like me
move with the wind.
I did lose all my pictures
from Vietnam. All that's gone.
Brings tears to my eyes.
My mother told me all these things
are going to happen. She said,
       "It's going to be hard
            sometimes, but you can't
stop and say, *I ain't gonna do this,
and I ain't gonna do tha*t."
I been on my own a long time.
Nobody but me to help me.
Everything I've seen to do, I've done.
The party was good. So what's left?
       Nothing. See a volcano and
            a tsunami. Die a happy man.

Emily Dygert
(artist)

1

Something I went through
was not survivor's guilt
but losing all those things
that supported a life.
In my book of business,
in my physical book of business,
I had lamp makers, ironworkers, really specific painters
that did the House of Blues,
people I met through different incarnations of me.
It was very difficult going through that book
and literally, physically, pulling out every card
and not knowing where people were,
just like, Where's it all gone?

When you talk about losses,
those are my greater losses,
the infrastructure of my life.
You have been stripped of everything
and have to go forward
totally naked in this new place,
mentally, emotionally, spiritually.
On the flip side, I never said,
Oh, it's terrible. I was in awe of
this hustling-bustling, shiny-beautiful city.
I saw the broad sky, the huge mountains,
and I just
            never looked back.

My house was two blocks off
the intersection of St. Charles and Napoleon
on the river side of St. Charles.
I went to the Contemporary Arts Center,
where I taught, and that's where
I slept during the storm.
Sixty-eight windows broke.
It flooded. Brick buildings crumbled
around it. So that was, in short,
my evacuation. When the wind
subsided, it was a war zone out there.
One of the big hotels with plate glass
windows looked bombed. Facades

blew off. This is what I call
the "dollhouse effect," where you could see in
all the rooms. Cars were smashed.
Refrigerators. Dead birds all over.
That's a picture of the aftermath.
Here you can see how high
the water went. This is a bent lamppost,
still working. This is a burnt-out car.
This is glass from the back of that car,
very, very melted. Here are more
refrigerators looking like they were dead.
This is the neighborhood I'd just moved to
looking so desolate. *No one there.*

During the storm you click into
some kind of mode. All this nature
comes out of people, good nature
and bad nature. I ended up getting stuck
in a situation where some people
I evacuated with decided I was pitting them
against each other . . . or conspiring
or something . . . Somehow this pervasive
negativity flowed through them,
person to person, and they ejected me,
just dropped me off curbside
at the airport. I remember one person—
her eyebrows were like this [frowns]

taping up my box: *You gotta leave right
now!* But whatever they did was good,
because it got me moving. Truly,
ultimately, I always seek the positive.
At this point, it's not cognitive.
I'm in survival mode.
I've got to pull it together.
Winston Churchill said—I love this—
"If you find yourself in hell,
keep going." Right?
You're in a hole? *Don't put up
curtains. Don't set up shop.*
I got to the airport. *No flights.*

There was military everywhere,
left and right, like being in some other
more militarized country. Well,
let me get a car. *No cars.*
Okay, what's my next plan of action?
Let me see who's going somewhere.
Are you going somewhere?
I was asking everyone and processing
step by step, taking everything in.
I thought, *There's a protective force
all around me. I have to tap into it.*
I conduct so much energy
that it has to flow out of me

to the outside, to everyone. This was about
creating a path through everything.
I recognize that the bigger picture
was about me being able to inspire people
through the experience of it.
Upon my return two months later,
I had a moving truck. I could have taken
tons of stuff, but in a very precious way
I just took what spoke to me,
which I placed in two very small boxes.
This picture is of me dancing in the street
with my friends my last night. You see
a lot of these "E's" on houses for "empty."

3

I moved to my last place in New Orleans
August 1, 2005. I moved into this studio
August 1, 2007. Very significant to me.
I've maintained my studio for a year and half
with virtually no connection to any system
in Phoenix. I've just kind of found things
along the way, stumbling and
moving forward, trying to regain footing.
I was adopted, so from the get-go,
I had to adapt. Upheaval is not
uncomfortable for me. I'm not sure who said,
In this world nothing can be said to be certain
except death and taxes. But to me,

change is certain. If things get to be
too stagnant, that's uncomfortable for me.
I have a deep rootedness in myself:
NAM-MYOHO-RENGE-KYO—
that's my Buddhist practice—
NAM-MYOHO-RENGE-KYO.
One, I have this natural ability.
Two, I have a creative mind,
and three, I think my practice allows me
to utilize all of those elements
to the best of my ability because
it is how and why I reconnect to
my own internal energy. I love to say

there's not good stuff and bad stuff,
just *stuff.* It's really what you do with it.
That's my life philosophy.
I have wanted to understand
how women use creative means.
One thing I found culturally is sewing.
I think that's very much a female art—
women making quilts and things.
In my contemporary, abstract way,
I tie that in by using threads, yarns and strings.
In this painting the canvas is sewn.
And that one, called "Beautiful Day,"
the one with the mountain and the sun.

I'm actually sewing into the painting,
moving right off the picture plane—
that idea of exploding into the environment.
I've incorporated two other elements
with sewing: mosaics and eggshells.
I love the texture of eggshells.
I'm more about painting, the process,
          the materials, the experience
more than the subject matter.
98% of the things here are pieces of my life
from different times in New Orleans.
This connects with the relationship I had.
This is from one of my early altars.

This is from my very last apartment.
A fourth element I forgot to mention is:
seeds. The hurricane spread seeds
into new areas. It's the idea of wind.
Those are real flower seeds
sewn into the painting. I'm creating
these patterns, like this one with circles.
Circles have continual, eternal energy.
To me, the egg is one of the simplest
symbols for life. It represents birth,
part of the cycle of life. I believe it's universally
recognizable. This will be in
my show, which is called "Rising from

the Wreckage: Putting the Pieces Back
Together." I have this
when you first walk in.
It's called "Broken,
          but not Broken."
I've got about twenty pieces.
This piece, this piece, and that piece there,
called "Movement," are four pieces
of an installation I'm going to suspend
so they hang across from each other,
forming a square. It's based on
the Buddhist concept that everything
in life has both an enlightened

and a defiled aspect, and with our own
conscious intention we can connect
with that enlightened aspect. I wanted
people to come in and physically
experience being closed in. This
is the working title, "There's Nothing
Inside." This is called "Tears,"
where I have literally, actually,
collected my tears and used them
in the painting. I'm still collecting tears,
and writing in conjunction
with my show. Here's a poem.
Do either of you speak Spanish?

La luna esta noche,
Es una canción.
Es un símbolo
De mi preparación
Para una vida nueva,
Con pasión y paz . . .
Mi vida nueva, es la luna . . . y más!
I knew as we were riding out of town
in that massive exodus, there was something
to go towards, something I was meant
to be doing. Here I am in Phoenix rising
        from the wreckage. Rising
                from the ashes like a phoenix.

Kid Merv, Some Jazz
(musician)

1

Saturday before the hurricane
my girlfriend went into labor.
Everybody's leaving town
and we're going uptown to Touro.
    My son was born
        at 2:13 a.m. Sunday morning
            and I was, Wow!
When he came out of the womb,
I went through years of music—
"Sunshine of my Life," James Brown,
Bob Marley, some jazz,
    "It's a Wonderful World," some
        Brass Band, Curtis Mayfield—
           the first songs he heard.
Monday morning, the hurricane
shattered windows on the top floors.
It's always said here, Hey,
if you're stuck in New Orleans,
    go to a hospital
        or St. Joe's "the bricks,"
           which are the Projects
which they're taking down,
the strong stuff. Anything else that's left—
this is my opinion—it's going to go.
It won't have a strong foundation.
    Anyway. Any disaster in the world
        you should have cash on you.
           We didn't have no cash.
We were there to have a baby.
We could not buy a $2 meal.
I said, I'll write you a check for $20.
No. You could be a millionaire,
    you're stuck in a disaster
        you can't do nothing.
           The world has crashed.

Monday night, there was a nice breeze.
We went for a walk with the baby
and could hear water everywhere—
shshshshshshshshshshshshsh—
                    but we couldn't see it.
                            We did not know
what was happening in the rest of the city.
All we had working was a radio,
people calling in to the Mayor,
saying, I'm on City Park Avenue
                    sitting on my porch.
                            No power, it's cool.
I got my barbeque on.
We have survived the storm.
Why is there water rising to my steps?
Is the levees . . . is the pumps on?
            The pumps are working, sir.
                    By 8:30 the same guy called back,
Why's the water still rising?
He didn't disrespect Mayor Nagin,
who was stalling, you know,
being who he is, knowing that
            he had a whole set
                    of people to move out,
as if we were all on *Survivor*.
Had it been in Nebraska or Idaho,
everybody would have been rescued,
given thousands of dollars to start over.

                    This is the land of the free.

2

Next day—oooh Lordy, it was hot—
the water reached us.
We had about 5 minutes to evacuate.
Katy wanted to go home,
and I said, What, are you crazy?
There's water everywhere.
We left with the clothes on our back.
A nurse stared at me, You Kid Merv?
You played at my friend's bachelor party.
I knew I knew you.
She took us to Baton Rouge.
We crossed the bridge, first thing
            she gets a flat. I go outside,
                    put my hands on the lugs,
                            and they're *hot hot hot*.
State troopers pull up.
They see a black man
changing a white woman's tire,
looked to them like a scam
or something. Racial profiling.
They go straight to the women,
Everything all right? I said, Look,
that's my baby in the car,
my baby's mother, and the nurse
that was taking care of my baby.
Oh, they said, you all all right?
No, we are not all right.
            I need some help with this tire!
                    Well you got to na na na na na

yourself. I was pissed, but I can trip.
We arrived Wed. night in Phoenix
and it was like a movie starring Us.
We were in Green Pastures.
It was beautiful. People
showed us around. This guy
heard me at Chances Are
and asked, May I help you?
I need a horn and some gigs.
So by Monday I had a horn. Valley Presbyterian
helped us with a nice little apartment, a car.
And that was it.
        We were here.
            I left everything.
I wanted to be right here with her,
for her. I think I was very thoughtful.
But we were going through a change.
A year today we're not together.
It's been rough. I was the type of guy
who'd have two gigs on Thursday,
three on Friday, five on Saturday.
Now I have a 12-month lease and no gigs.
I don't know what God
has in store for me,
but I'm here for a reason.
        I can survive. We've
            all been through it.

3

I have a CD to put out
with Mr. Ellis Marsalis on piano.
I called him up, asked if he would help me.
Sure. What more can I ask for? Lord
'a mercy. I'm singing with top-of-the-line guys.
               But it's a Monopoly thing right now,
                         Do not go past Go.
                                   Do not collect $200.
I lost my pal here this year, Frederick Shepard.
He was a big brother to me, kept my sanity.
I went to New Orleans for 6 months
to help my mother out with some things.
He said, Man, don't you ever leave me again.
               I'm not going to leave you,
                         I promise, it's me and you, kid.
I thought, That's a switch. I was the Kid.
Shepp said, Nobody in New Orleans
knows what you really can do.
You see, I come up through the old tradition.
Started on the horn at 11, youngest member
               of the Brass Band at 13.
                         That's the way we did it.
Last time I saw Shepp, he was singing,
Do do dee dee da zu zu zu za.
What's the name of that song?
Amigo. What's the name of that song?
Amigo. That means "great friend."
               I thought he meant
                         I was his great friend,
Do do dee dee da zu zu zu za.
He'd said, Don't leave me, but he left me.
I'm writing a song for my son,
Hector, named for my father,
a Jamaican merchant seaman, died
               when I was 11.
                         Never heard me play.

               I'm calling the song, *Has Anyone Seen Hector?*

Sally Cole
(writer)

1

I was going. My son, Davie, and Angela
were going. But Catherine would not go.
I was on the phone it seemed like forever.
"I have four cats and two carriers."

Throw your cats in the car.
"It's going to turn." *Come with me*
to Baton Rouge. "Don't worry."
Thursday before Katrina, Catherine took me for Lasik,

which I'd been planning to do. Afterwards,
I had my little Ambien pills and eye guards,
and went right to bed at 4 p.m.
Friday I woke up at 4 a.m. with *vision.*

I was so high that I sat on my porch
looking and looking at the streetlights glowing.
The whole world was new.
By Saturday, I'm evacuating,

putting eye drops in as I drive,
feeling like a rat for abandoning Catherine.
She'd said, "It'll turn. I'll be fine."
I gave up. Left her to her fate.

2

In Baton Rouge, the woman next door
for some reason had cable,
and kept coming by going,
You can't believe it!
"Anything about Lakeview?" *Ooooh*,
she'd say. When our TV came back on,
I saw where New Orleans flooded.
I used to run along Pontchartrain
on the levee they filled with sand.
                                        So I knew.

Sunday I headed for D.C.
When I pulled in to a Subway in Roanoke,
my cell phone rang (504 numbers
hadn't worked all week). My son
Chris said: *The Coast Guard rescued Catherine*!
I burst into tears as the server asked,
Would you like cheese?
I hadn't known I was so tense.
Nights I'd clenched my jaw
so hard a tooth cracked.

Chris's girlfriend took me in
to her beautiful house in Woodley Park.
I woke to weird dogs, barking.
Not dogs but gibbons
in the zoo set off each morning by
the sirens of Dick Cheney's motorcade
on Connecticut Avenue. Davie's computer
had a satellite program so I could find
how high the floodwaters rose.
I typed my address: 6229 Memphis.

Water level 9.9 feet.
I typed in Mike's address:
Zero point zero.
There is no God.
After a month, Lakeview residents could go back
to look and leave. Oh my god oh my
god. *The whole thing was surreal.*
We all used that word, "surreal."
I salvaged whatever, which was nothing,
except my dishes.

Black, splotchy mold everywhere.
Everything dead, a horrible gray
you've never seen. A smell
you can't imagine. Fuzzy, lime green
and salmon-colored mold covering
your home. Eerily beautiful, sort of
fascinating. "What's this squishy—?"
I was walking on pulpy . . . books.
Everywhere: *books, books, books.*
Oh, oh, this was my house

I bought myself.
I should have packed my mother's stuff
that she left me, her yearbook from WWII—
she was a WASP, Women's Air Service Pilot—
and, Oh, I didn't think of Kate away at college,
who started writing at seven,
a lifetime of journals under her bed.
All pulp now. My pictures, pulp.
And nowhere the feral cat I fed
that would come through my dog's—

my ex-dog's—door flap,
to eat and scoot back out
and never let me touch her.
My neighbor had a cross with an arrow
sprayed on the house.
I thought, *That's strange*,
and then looked down:
a small mound of black fur.
The animal part of the storm—
I just can't even think about it.

Insurance adjusters are the scum of the earth.
They eat their young.
They nickled and dimed us to death.
I'd call them every day
like a part-time job. And wait.
Finally, I'd had enough.
"Just give me my check."
I had a post office box.
New Orleans was a ghost town.
No mailmen because no houses,

but Farmers sends my check to 6229 Memphis!
They did it on purpose. They were evil.
They were *all* evil. If I kept moving,
I was okay. I put 10,000 miles on my car.
In New York I was at a light near Gramercy Park
and a young couple asked directions.
"Don't ask me. I'm from New Orleans."
"We are too!" "How'd you do?"
That's what you'd ask. *How'd you do?*
"Lost everything." *So did I.*

3

I'm very lucky. I stayed
at my family's cabin in the woods
until I bought in Tucson last year. One night
I walked back from my neighbor's,

and came into a clearing and went [gasps].
It's an *un*believable sky in Flag.
The stars. The huge Milky Way.
I took a deep breath, and [gasps],

fell. Just about—God!
Hit a rock. Blood all over me.
When I returned to New Orleans,
I told a friend how I looked up at the night sky

and lost my balance,
and she said, Katrina Falling Syndrome.
Nancy and Kathy, Tim Stan and me: we all fell.
We weren't at the Superdome. We

didn't lose family. We
hurt ourselves because we
didn't suffer enough. I only
stayed two days it was so creepy.

No animals, no birds, no ants, no roaches,
no beetles. Or children. The children
were all gone, like Hamlen Town.
I thought, *I gotta get out of here*.

After the divorce, I was in a rut. I mean,
New Orleans was great. I liked my job,
my house. I had a kid living nearby.
But then, I got set free.

Freddie Munn, Jr.
(auto mechanic, retired)

The part that they showed on TV
is where I come from.
Right there. Lower and Upper
Ninth Ward. When the rain came,
it rained and rained,
            and the wind was so strong
                    it pulled up the big, old trees—
I'm talking three-hundred-year-old trees—
like they was nothing and blew them
blocks away. When the storm came,
the water was deep but clear.
When the levee broke, everything backed up.
            Then the water come
                    like a tidal wave
pushing houses off their foundations . . .
bam bam bam. The locks were closed
but water came underneath . . . *boom boom boom.*
I was in my wheelchair and the water
was this height. I said, Uh-oh,
            we gotta get out of here.
                    We made a raft of doors,
and tied my wheelchair down.
You could see that water coming. *Whoa.*
I never panicked. I never was scared.
I was prepared, pleased I could swim.
When I fell in and went down,
            I relaxed and come back up,
                    then started swimming.

The water turned icky–full
of sewage and dead animals.
I swam the whole way
and my brother rolled my chair up
on the Claiborne overpass.
                    That's where we stayed
                              for seven days.
Everybody got diarrhea,
and people with open sores
got bubbles on their legs.
You could hear the houses in New Orleans
collapse. All night the sound of crying.
            Dogs barking,
                        cats screaming.
On the third day, helicopters come
with rations. By then people was delirious.
We had reporters taking pictures.
They come right up to the bridge.
I said, *Give us water*. They took my picture.
            Finally, they began
                        to airlift the sick.
One woman had cried all night
'cause she ran out of her arthritis medicine.
They told her the harness was safe.
She was a big lady, maybe 250 lbs.
She got all the way up to the helicopter
            and then she fell.
                  Her body hit
the bridge like an accordion.
I think, personally, with the constant pain,
she tired of living.
She had lost her home,
her city, her health.
            She just wanted to go.
                  People say, *move on*.
It's hard when you've lost everything.
I wore out on the seventh day.
I didn't think I would make it.
I thought the water would go back down,
but it never moved. *It never moved*.

I would like to elaborate on the stories
about the murders and the rapes in the Superdome.
People had been there four days without food
or water. They was trying to get out.
They were told to come to the Superdome
              and they did. Then nobody
                        let them leave. Those babies
died from malnutrition.
No water, no food.
It was survival of the fittest.
That's what it was.
The fascinating part is that people
              from Saudi Arabia, Russia,
                        wanted to send doctors.
Some folks came with their own money—
three big trucks with medical supplies—
but the head of FEMA wouldn't let them
in the city. He had a big old power struggle
with the governor who was fighting
              with the mayor, but the mayor
                        does not control the levees.
The federal government is in charge of the levees.
There's a big old lawsuit going on right now,
but ain't nobody going to take responsibility.
We asked the guys who come to get us,
What took you so long?
              When they got to us,
                        it was too late.
I knew a lot of the people died.
They had one lady on the phone
they had told to
(I was listening on the radio)
cut a hole in the roof
              and climb out with her baby.
                        There's 100-degree heat
in those attics! 99% humidity!
The foundation gave way.
They found her with the baby
cradled by her body
as if to protect it.

When we got here,
everybody talking about
starting over. Let me tell you,
            it ain't easy.
                        Ain't nobody
to help me. I *asked* for help,
but the FEMA representative who
interviewed me said I was too
            independent. Gal, I said,
                        you ought to encourage
people to be independent.
FEMA hired contract workers
to file our cases and that one
            frauded FEMA numbers
                        so her family got our
checks. Many of us was frauded
this way, and we have been *ignored*.
Why? Some of us scammed
            are struggling so hard
                        and cannot get help with
necessary things that life requires,
or retrieve us some dignity
and happiness possible
            with all the sadness of separation
                        from our families and lifelong friends.

I been in a wheelchair
with a spinal cord injury
since my car accident in '83.
        I can tell the ones
              that learn how to be
self-reliant. If they're not,
they don't live long, trust me.
They break down. They try to resume
        their life as it was,
              and in actual reality
it takes five years for your body
to come back to where you have
some kind of control over it.
        The mind got to be refocused.
           You got to change your friends.
I am the "only paraplegic/handicapped
individual" to graduate from
the Arizona Automotive Institute.
        I have the drive
           to help myself since
the government can't seem to do me right.
When I see people that needs help, I say,
Don't take the easy way out.
        Keep yourself from the negative.
           That's what I'm talking about.

List of
Plates

James Davidson
(artist)

Jim, in the living room of his new home, purchased after Hurricane Katrina, Tempe, Arizona, March 2009

Front steps, Jim's Louisiana home, New Orleans, Louisiana, November 2008

Front door with trees, Jim's Louisiana home, New Orleans, Louisiana, November 2008

The bedroom in Jim's new home, Tempe, Arizona, March 2009

The wisteria Jim could see every day, New Orleans, Louisiana, November 2008

The sidewalk in front of Jim's Louisiana home, New Orleans, Louisiana, November 2008

Jim's bedroom window, Tempe, Arizona, March 2009

Jade figurine from Jim's Louisiana home, Tempe, Arizona, March 2009

Deborah Green
(Winn-Dixie employee: meat department, retired)

Deborah, outside her apartment, where she moved with her son after Hurricane Katrina, Phoenix, Arizona, April 2008

The place where Deborah's house stood before Hurricane Katrina, New Orleans, Louisiana, November 2008

Deborah's photo album, salvaged after Hurricane Katrina, Phoenix, Arizona, April 2008

Enclosure, New Orleans, Louisiana, November 2008

Miriam Youngerman Miller
(professor emerita)

Mimi, in the living room of her patio home, purchased after she left New Orleans, Tempe, Arizona, November 2008

The street where Mimi lived, New Orleans, Louisiana, November 2008

 Mimi's former home, New Orleans, Louisiana, November 2008

 Down the street from Mimi's house, New Orleans, Louisiana, November 2008

 Mimi, at the front gate of her new home, Tempe, Arizona, November 2008

Victoria Green
(mother of four)

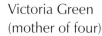 Victoria, in her living room (her fourth move after Hurricane Katrina), Minneapolis, Minnesota, November 2009

 The neighborhood market near where Victoria's family lived for three generations (#2), New Orleans, Louisiana, November 2008

 The neighborhood market near where Victoria's family lived for three generations (#1), New Orleans, Louisiana, November 2008

The neighborhood market near where Victoria's family lived for three generations (#3), New Orleans, Louisiana, November 2008

The neighborhood market near where Victoria's family lived for three generations (#4), New Orleans, Louisiana, November 2008

Untitled, New Orleans, Louisiana, November 2008

Lawanda and Sean Scott
(administrative assistant, fire alarm dispatcher)

Lawanda and Sean, in the dining room of Lawanda's mother's home, repaired after Hurricane Katrina, New Orleans, Louisiana, December 2009

Looking out the front door, Lawanda's mother's home, New Orleans, Louisiana, December 2009

Side yard, Lawanda's mother's home, New Orleans, Louisiana, December 2009

Sean, holding his and Lawanda's wedding video, the only video left in their apartment by the looters after Hurricane Katrina, New Orleans, Louisiana, December 2009

Front door of Lawanda's mother's home, repaired after Hurricane Katrina, New Orleans, Louisiana, December 2009

Catherine Loomis
(professor)

Sidewalk near Catherine's home, New Orleans, Louisiana, November 2008

Untitled, New Orleans, Louisiana, November 2008

The porch where Catherine sat every day before being rescued by helicopter after Hurricane Katrina, New Orleans, Louisiana, November 2008

My parents' refrigerator, in their side yard after Hurricane Ike, Houston, Texas, October 2008

Catherine, in the reading room of her upstairs duplex, New Orleans, Louisiana, November 2008

The staircase to Catherine's apartment, New Orleans, Louisiana, November 2008

Ardiss "Ardie" Cooper (Direct Hit at Diamondhead, Mississippi)
(casino bartender)

Ardie, in the living room of her new apartment, where she moved after Hurricane Katrina, Scottsdale, Arizona, April 2009

The only jewelry Ardie was able to save from Hurricane Katrina, Scottsdale, Arizona, April 2009

The box of pictures and letters that Ardie took with her after Hurricane Katrina struck, Scottsdale, Arizona, April 2009

Richard Lyons
(Vietnam veteran)

Richard, in front of his third apartment after Hurricane Katrina, Phoenix, Arizona, April 2009

The Claiborne Avenue Bridge, seen from the Lower Ninth Ward, New Orleans, Louisiana, December 2009

Emily Dygert
(artist)

From the two boxes of objects Emily gathered after Hurricane Katrina, Emily's studio floor, Phoenix, Arizona, November 2008

Bench with Aspidistra, New Orleans, Louisiana, November 2008

Untitled, New Orleans, Louisiana, November 2008

Untitled, New Orleans, Louisiana, November 2008

Emily, in her studio, Phoenix, Arizona, November 2008

Kid Merv
(musician)

Kid Merv, playing his trumpet on the hotel balcony, Tempe, Arizona, October 2007

Kid Merv's hotel room, Tempe, Arizona, October 2007

Kid Merv, playing his trumpet, Tempe, Arizona, October 2007

Kid Merv, on the morning after his gig, Tempe, Arizona, October 2007

Kid Merv's trumpet, Tempe, Arizona, October 2007

Sally Cole
(writer)

The empty lot where Sally's home stood before Hurricane Katrina, New Orleans, Louisiana, November 2008

Prickly pear cactus with fruit, Sally's front yard, Tucson, Arizona, June 2009

Address marker saved from Sally's razed Louisiana home, Tucson, Arizona, June 2009

Dusk at Sally's new home, Tucson, Arizona, June 2009

Sally, in the front yard of her new home, purchased four years after Hurricane Katrina, Tucson, Arizona, June 2009

Freddie Munn, Jr.
(auto mechanic, retired)

The Claiborne Avenue Bridge, where Freddie stayed for seven days after Hurricane Katrina, New Orleans, Louisiana, November 2008

The house where Freddie lived before Hurricane Katrina, New Orleans, Louisiana, December 2009

Freddie, in his new apartment after Hurricane Katrina, Phoenix, Arizona, April 2008

Acknowledgments

To the Hurricane Katrina evacuees who shared their travails and triumphs, their life-journeys with us: this book is a tribute to you, to your courage and fortitude, creativity and resourcefulness, spirit and soul. Thank you.

Thanks to the editors of the following journals for publishing individual interview-poems, some in conjunction with individual photographs, and sometimes in earlier versions and with other titles: *42Opus*: "Richard Lyons," "Sally Cole"; *Bayou*: "Victoria Green (mother of four)"; *Bosphorus Art Project Quarterly*: "Freddie Munn, Jr."; *Cutthroat*: "Catherine Loomis"; *EPR*: "Ardiss 'Ardie' Cooper (Direct Hit at Diamondhead, Mississippi)"; *Exquisite Corpse*: "Kid Merv, Some Jazz" (full-length); *Frontiers*: "Deborah Green" (excerpt); *Journal of Southern Religion*: "Kid Merv, Some Jazz" (excerpt); *Kestrel*: "Emily Dygert"; *The Drunken Boat*: "James Davidson," "Miriam Youngerman Miller." Thanks to the Centre for Contemporary Art and the Natural World in Exeter, UK, director Clive Adams, and curator Elizabeth-Jane Burnett, for including the following interview-poems and photographs in the exhibit, *Skylines: Ecopoetics*: "Catherine Loomis," "Victoria Green," "James Davidson," "Sally Cole."

Two funded faculty leaves from the Department of English at Arizona State University afforded Cynthia Hogue time to work on this book. A Residency Fellowship from the MacDowell Colony helped her to advance it. Support from the Arizona Commission on the Arts, city of Tempe, Arizona, the Maxine and Jonathan Marshall Chair in Modern and Contemporary Poetry at Arizona State University, and the Ted Decker Catalyst Fund afforded Hogue and Rebecca Ross the funding to bring this project into being as both exhibit and book. A Creative Writing Faculty Enrichment Grant from the Virginia G. Piper Center for Creative Writing at Arizona State University crucially supported the preparation of a manuscript that included fine art photography. We are grateful to all these organizations for this support.

Cynthia Hogue and Rebecca Ross are grateful to our editor, Bill Lavender, for his steadfast interest in and support of our project. We are also grateful to all those who helped further this project along the way: Christopher Burawa, Shelley Cohn, Roy Flukinger, Catherine Hammond, Neal Lester, Dan Mayer, Jessica Munns, Alberto Ríos, Lupita Barron-Ríos, Alan Michael Parker, Rebecca Seiferle, Peggy Shumaker, Ron Smith, Peter Turchi, Afaa Michael Weaver, and Shelly White. Thanks to Hogue's Research Assistants, the poets Claire McQuerry, Katie Cappello, Mark Haunschild, and Kathleen Winter, for their help with all aspects of the book.

Special thanks to Ted Decker for support and assistance with grants, Eddie Shea for book design, Dan Vermillion and Michael Lundgren of Sonoran Print Editions, for their advice and attention to detail as they prepared scans and digital files for the book and exhibits. Thanks also to city of Tempe Cultural Services, especially Adrienne Richwine, Maja Aurora, Elizabeth Lagman, and Rachael Peterson, the city of Tempe Municipal Arts Commission, and Rebecca Bond of Tempe Connections. Great gratitude goes to Robert Sanders, Community, Family & Congregations Program Manager for Lutheran Social Services of the Southwest, for so generously talking to evacuees about this project and asking preliminarily whether they might speak with Hogue about their experiences. His steadfast belief in this project has been crucial.

Thanks to the following individuals and institutions for hosting initial exhibitions of the interview-poems and photographs in conjunction with the publication of this book: Pinna Joseph, Changing Hands Bookstore, and Colleen Jennings-Roggensack and Brad Myers, ASU Gammage, supported by grants from the city of Tempe; Dianne Cripe, city of Goodyear; and Valerie Vadala Homer and Wendy Raisanen of Scottsdale Public Art, supported by the Scottsdale Cultural Council.

Especially, we thank our families, Sylvain Gallais, Paul Morris, Bob and Polly Ross, and Ross Morris, for their patience and support as we undertook this project.

Authors' Note

This collection of images and words has grown out of an extended collaboration among writer, photographer, and each of the Hurricane Katrina evacuees we interviewed and photographed. Although the individual poems and photographs are deeply rooted in the documentary tradition, we do not claim to present a single truth or judgment. Instead, our intent is to share the personal experiences of a handful of Katrina evacuees, as individuals representative of the many people affected by this tragedy. We seek through our art to create a space for voices to be heard and people to be seen who might otherwise be invisible or forgotten. In this sense, we act as witnesses, communicating what we have seen and heard, filtered through our own perceptions and aesthetics.

The poems are drawn from the actual words of the evacuees, all of whom landed at some point in one place among many across the United States. (In the case of those interviewed for this book, that place was Arizona.) All poems have been shaped and edited out of the original interviews, some of which were fifty-pages long once transcribed. Nothing has been added.

The photographer and evacuees created the portraits together, primarily in their Arizona homes. Sometimes, the photographer traveled to reconnect with evacuees who continued to migrate throughout the country, as far north as Minnesota and as far south as Louisiana, as they settled into new lives after the storm. Other photographs record everyday details of these people's lives—repaired, dilapidated, or razed houses; native plants and foliage in both Louisiana and Arizona; personal items saved from the storm.

In one case, creative license was used in the selection of photographs for this book. While photographing at her parents' home after Hurricane Ike, the photographer recalled many unsettling echoes of the stories told to her by the Katrina evacuees. By including one photograph from the aftermath of Hurricane Ike, Ross blended the experiences of two storms into one.

These interview-poems and photographs stand as individual facets of a larger mosaic. Together, they begin a conversation. The photographs and words presented here are used with the evacuees' permission.

Cynthia Hogue and Rebecca Ross
www.WhenTheWaterCame.com

About the Authors

In 1991, Cynthia Hogue moved to take a job in New Orleans, a city to which she was a complete foreigner and a culture to which she was an unwilling newcomer. She weathered Hurricane Andrew her second year, along with most residents of the city who stayed to wait out the storm. There was no evacuation plan, and only one road out of town. So many plans, logistically complicated but practically necessary, were left for another day in "the city that care forgot." When Hogue left New Orleans four years later, however, she had seen in action a real, if imperfect, effort to make a great and beautiful city truly multicultural, and she never forgot. It is in memory of that city that this project was born.

Cynthia Hogue is currently Professor and Maxine and Jonathan Marshall Chair in Modern and Contemporary Poetry at Arizona State University. She has published ten books, including the co-edited *Innovative Women Poets: An Anthology of Contemporary Poetry and Interviews*, and six collections of poetry, most recently, *The Incognito Body* (2006) and *Or Consequence* (2010), both with Red Hen Press. Among her honors are a 2009 Witter Bynner Translation Residency at the Santa Fe Art Institute, MacDowell Colony and Wurlitzer Foundation residencies, an Artist Project Grant from the Arizona Commission on the Arts, a Fulbright-Hayes Fellowship, and a National Endowment for the Arts Fellowship in poetry.

Growing up in Houston, Texas, Rebecca Ross experienced more than her fair share of hurricanes. During one particular storm, she traveled from her grandfather's house in her parents' car through darkness so intensified by rain and wind that she lay along the car floorboard until safely reaching home. After Hurricane Katrina, she began the process of helping her parents prepare to move from Texas to Arizona. She coordinated repairs to their home after Hurricane Ike sent a tree through the bedroom, helped sell the family house and farm, then relocated her parents to their new Arizona home. During these many months, she often thought of the Katrina evacuees' stories and recognized the great luxury her parents had, being able methodically to go through their possessions, deciding what to take or leave, as they willingly made their first move in forty-five years.

Rebecca Ross's photographs have been exhibited throughout the United States and in Europe at venues such as the Eye Gallery, San Francisco; Society for Contemporary Photography, Kansas City; and Canon Photo Gallery, Amsterdam. She has completed several public art projects in Arizona and has received recognition from the Scottsdale Cultural Council and Center in Santa Fe for her teaching and outreach work with disadvantaged youth. Her photographs are represented in public and private collections including the Museum of Fine Arts–Houston, Phoenix Office of Arts and Culture, Mayo Clinic–Scottsdale, and the Harry Ransom Center in Austin, Texas. Her awards include an individual Artist Fellowship and Artist Project Grant from the Arizona Commission on the Arts.

Also Available from UNO Press:

William Christenberry: Art & Family by J. Richard Gruber (2000)

The El Cholo Feeling Passes by Fredrick Barton (2003)

A House Divided by Fredrick Barton (2003)

Coming Out the Door for the Ninth Ward edited by Rachel Breunlin, from The Neighborhood Story Project series (2006)

The Change Cycle Handbook by Will Lannes (2008)

Cornerstones: Celebrating the Everyday Monuments & Gathering Places of New Orleans edited by Rachel Breunlin, from The Neighborhood Story Project series (2008)

A Gallery of Ghosts by John Gery (2008)

Hearing Your Story: Songs of History and Life for Sand Roses by Nabile Farès, translated by Peter Thompson, from The Engaged Writers Series (2008)

The Imagist Poem: Modern Poetry in Miniature edited by William Pratt, from The Ezra Pound Center for Literature series (2008)

The Katrina Papers: A Journal of Trauma and Recovery by Jerry W. Ward, Jr., from The Engaged Writers Series (2008)

On Higher Ground: The University of New Orleans at Fifty by Dr. Robert Dupont (2008)

Us Four Plus Four: Eight Russian Poets Conversing translated by Don Mager (2008)

Voices Rising: Stories from the Katrina Narrative Project edited by Rebeca Antoine (2008)

Gravestones (Lápidas) by Antonio Gamoneda, translated by Donald Wellman, from The Engaged Writers Series (2009)

The House of Dance and Feathers: A Museum by Ronald W. Lewis by Rachel Breunlin & Ronald W. Lewis, from The Neighborhood Story Project series (2009)

I hope it's not over, and good-by: Selected Poems of Everette Maddox by Everette Maddox (2009)

Portraits: Photographs in New Orleans 1998-2009 by Jonathan Traviesa (2009)

Theoretical Killings: Essays & Accidents by Steven Church (2009)

Voices Rising II: More Stories from the Katrina Narrative Project edited by Rebeca Antoine (2010)

Rowing to Sweden: Essays on Faith, Love, Politics, and Movies by Fredrick Barton (2010)

Dogs in My Life: The New Orleans Photographs of John Tibule Mendes (2010)

Understanding the Music Business: A Comprehensive View edited by Harmon Greenblatt & Irwin Steinberg (2010)

The Fox's Window by Naoko Awa, translated by Toshiya Kamei (2010)

A Passenger from the West by Nabile Farés, translated by Peter Thompson, from The Engaged Writers Series (2010)

The Schüssel Era in Austria: Contemporary Austrian Studies, Volume 18 edited by Günter Bischof & Fritz Plasser (2010)

The Gravedigger by Rob Magnuson Smith (2010)

Everybody Knows What Time It Is by Reginald Martin (2010)

Aunt Alice Vs. Bob Marley by Kareem Kennedy, from The Neighborhood Story Project series (2010)

Houses of Beauty: From Englishtown to the Seventh Ward by Susan Henry, from The Neighborhood Story Project series (2010)

Signed, The President by Kenneth Phillips, from The Neighborhood Story Project series (2010)

Beyond the Bricks by Daron Crawford & Pernell Russell, from The Neighborhood Story Project series (2010)

Green Fields: Crime, Punishment, & a Boyhood Between by Bob Cowser, Jr., from the Engaged Writers Series (2010)

http://unopress.uno.edu